The Sacrament Is for Me

Written by Jessica B. Ellingson • Illustrated by Chase Jensen

CFI • An Imprint of Cedar Fort, Inc.
Springville, Utah

To Claire, Lindzie, Quinten, Ryker, Ezra, Annie, and Macy for inspiring this book.
—Jessica

To my wife, Ashley, and my daughters Adalyn and Brielle. Thank you for always making sacrament meeting interesting.
—Chase

Text © 2016 Jessica B. Ellingson
Illustrations © 2016 Chase Jensen
All rights reserved.

ISBN 13: 978-1-4621-1880-9

Published by CFI, an imprint of Cedar Fort, Inc.
2373 W. 700 S., Springville, UT 84663
Distributed by Cedar Fort, Inc., www.cedarfort.com

Library of Congress Control Number: 2016942346

Cover design and typesetting by Shawnda T. Craig
Cover design © 2016 Cedar Fort, Inc.
Edited by Chelsea Holdaway

Printed in the United States of America

10 9 8 7 6 5 4 3 2 1

Printed on acid-free paper

We get to take the SACRAMENT
To start off every week.

With FOLDED ARMS
and EYES now CLOSED,
We HEAR the SACRED PRAYERS.

They tell us of CHRIST'S
flesh and blood
HE GAVE because HE CARES.

The WATER is symbolic of
The BLOOD CHRIST SHED for all

While He PRAYED in GETHSEMANE
And SAVED US from the Fall.

The priests BREAK BREAD
to represent
The SUFFERING He bore

When JESUS CHRIST was CRUCIFIED
So we COULD LIVE once more.

The bread, the water,
and the prayers
REMIND US of the price,

So while they pass the sacrament,
BE CAREFUL HOW YOU ACT.

IT'S NOT A TIME for being rough
Or munching on a snack.

It's not a time to play with toys
Or pull your sister's hair.

Instead we try to think of Him
WITH REVERENCE, LOVE, AND CARE.

He offers us ETERNAL LIFE,
Forever families.

We only need to
FOLLOW HIM,
And TRUST in His decrees.

He showed us how
to be BAPTIZED,
RECEIVE the HOLY GHOST.

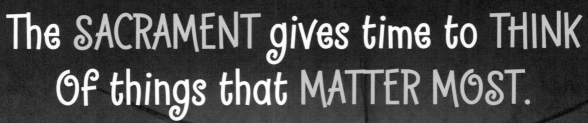

The SACRAMENT gives time to THINK
Of things that MATTER MOST.

We promise to REMEMBER HIM,
To take and SHARE HIS NAME,
And through example
spread His word,
TELL OTHERS why He came.

We try to be like JESUS CHRIST
And GIVE our LOVE to all

By kindly SERVING those we know
In ways both BIG and SMALL.

Our Father up in HEAVEN above
WILL GUIDE US on our way

And that is why the SACRAMENT
Is WONDERFUL to me.

It lets me start a brand-new week
With special EYES TO SEE . . . .

The SIMPLE THINGS that I must do
To SERVE with all my might.

The SACRAMENT will
HELP US know
How we can
CHOOSE THE RIGHT.

~ About the AUTHOR ~

JESSICA B. ELLINGSON

Jessica grew up in a small town in southeastern Utah and moved to Utah County to attend college. After graduating with her bachelor's degree, she pursued her dream of becoming a book editor. She now lives above the valley with her cave-dweller husband and is pursuing another dream of becoming an author.

~ About the ILLUSTRATOR ~

CHASE JENSEN

Chase grew up in Cleveland, Utah, and has always wanted to be an artist. He went to Brigham Young University where he studied illustration. He later returned to live near his small hometown with his wife and two daughters. You can find his work at www.chasejensenart.com.

Sleep Tight!

By Constance Allen
Illustrated by David Prebenna

A SESAME STREET/GOLDEN PRESS BOOK
Published by Western Publishing Company, Inc.,
in conjunction with Children's Television Workshop.

© 1991 Children's Television Workshop. Sesame Street puppet characters © 1991 Jim Henson Productions, Inc. All rights reserved. Printed in the U.S.A. No part of this book may be reproduced or copied in any form without written permission from the publisher. Sesame Street and the Sesame Street sign are registered trademarks and service marks of Children's Television Workshop. All other trademarks are the property of Western Publishing Company, Inc. Library of Congress Catalog Card Number: 90-84467 ISBN: 0-307-10026-X/ ISBN: 0-307-66026-5 (lib. bdg.) MCMXCI A

"Time to go home, Elmo!" calls Elmo's daddy.

"Just one more game of monster tag, please,
Daddy?" says Elmo.

"OK. One more game," says Elmo's daddy.

On the way home from the park,
Elmo and his daddy see lots of other people
on their way home, too.
It's almost bedtime for little monsters.

EAT AT
JOE'S

CLOSED

On Sesame Street, everyone is getting ready for bed.
Splish, splash!
Little Bird shakes his feathers in his warm bath.

Sleepy monsters comb their fur and brush their teeth.

Flossie isn't sleepy yet. Herry and Flossie do jumping jacks.

"... Seven! Eight! Nine! Ten!" pants Herry Monster. "Are you getting sleepy, Flossie?" Flossie shakes her head.

"Ten toe touches!" says Herry. "One! Two! Three! Four ..."

Oscar finishes his book, *Mother Grouch Rhymes*.
"Little Boy Grouch, come blow your kazoo.
Take a mud bath and eat anchovy stew . . ."
He closes his book.
Sleep tight, sleepy grouch.

Big Bird sings his teddy bear a lullaby.
   "Rock-a-bye, Radar, snug in my nest.
   Time for us both to lie down and rest!
"Sleep tight, little bear," says Big Bird.

At the Snuffleupagus's cave,
it's bedtime for Alice.
Boing! Boing! Boing!
She bounces on the bed.
Sleep tight, Alice.

In the Count's castle, the Count counts sheep.
"One sheep! Two sheep! Three beautiful, woolly
sheep!" cries the Count.
Sleep tight, Count.

In the country, Cowboy Grover settles down to sleep under the stars.
"Sleep tight, little cows!" he calls.

In the city, Hoots the Owl plays a saxophone serenade above the city lights.

Bee-boop-a-diddly-diddly-doo-wah-doo!

"I'll keep things cool till morning," he croons. "Sleep tight, everybody."

In Ernie's window box, sleepy twiddlebugs
snuggle under their leaf blankets.
Sleep tight, little twiddlebugs.

All is quiet on Sesame Street. Monsters and birds and grouches and twiddlebugs sleep soundly in their beds.

Sleep tight, little Elmo.